THE HIDDEN SECRET OF SUCCESSFUL INTERNATIONAL BUSINESSES & COMPANIES

(COMPANIES, IMPORT & EXPORT, BAKING AND INTERNATIONAL TRADES/LOCAL TRADES)

CHRIS THANKGOD

DEDICATION

I dedicate this book to Chris Thankgod's family, friends,wel-wisher and as many that want to become Business jagerband, and as well going far in Business

CONTENTS

PREFACE

The aim of writing this book is to help business owners and traders of different kinds to have a stress free business life and help them know the profit, capital and many more in business. Also it makes them to know and enjoy the benefits of their toiling in the business they are into or about to start.

INTRODUCTION

This book teaches business owners [importers and exporters, companies owners and many who are into small scale trading] how to manage and start up a business without falling for business breakdown such as financial challenge, rise and falling of capital and lost but rather knowing your profit and many more in business. In this book business owners learn or know the strategies of making 100 – 500 Trillion, Billions, Millions and Thousands in your currency and as well in Dollar's in a day. This book will teach you how to embark on a business you don't know with the little ideas you have and how to run your business without being cheated and your goods not staying too long in your way house or store. Some business owners are meeting the demand of the amount listed [making 100 – 500 Trillion, Billions, Millions and Thousands in your currency and as well in Dollar's in a day] but can't give an account or knowing the income and outcome of their business and knowing where and when to put finance in their business as well as how to take money in their business [how much to collect and how much to put] this book will teach you all of this

CHAPTER 1

These are some of the hidden secrets or strategy that companies don't know or I may say these are some minor hidden secrets that falls companies unknown to them, but they keep on thinking that the business is not flowing well (there is no enough customers) or there is rise of capital (market cost price is high) that is why they can't meet up, some advisers will say "the result of their business downfall is because they don't know the business they are doing that's the result of their business downfall". Now let me ask these silly questions how did you want to know the business? Secondly; baking for example, you knowing how to bake or knowing the processes of baking will it make your business not to fall or prevent a cheat from your workers and managers or will it reduce the number of worker? The answer is no, you knowing it won't prevent all of these things or reduce the workers you are suppose to use. Now I ask again, why is it that you know all the process of the business yet market cost price still fall your company or business down, that is to say none of all these are the causes of company or business down fall, but these minor things fall and collapse companies and business because they don't take them serious or see them as something, but these little things I will state out are the headache to our businesses and companies. INGREDENT, MARKETING PRICE, WORK SCHEDULE AND SPLITION: you might look at it, as something not meaningful or not necessary but believe me it is. You buying in large quantities, in bulks or in retails doesn't matter, what matter is, is your company or business growing or falling (increasing or reducing)? Are you seeing your gain as expected or you're using more than your gain? If reducing, then know that someday it will come to nothing and your business or company will collapse because that small small lose you are losing makes up your downfall. A business or company owner (boss) who doesn't know the number of items he or she produce or baked is band to fall, like wise to an owner who doesn't know splition (cost price, selling price and gain) is band to fall, some companies or business make a guess price to sell their product because of their cost price. E.g. I produce or baked biscuits with $ 50, so I'll make a guessing price of $ 50, that is why we are easily beaten by other company or business, and our goods or products stayed long in the ware house.

.

CHAPTER 2
INGREDIENT

INGREDIENT: This is the primary items or root functions of any producing goods or products. These are one of the basic things a business or company owner must know, in other to be a successful company or business owner (rising and falling of his or her business or company).

As a company or business owner, is your duty to know the cost price of every items and the amount of goods produced out of those items. For example, I owned a company that manufactures phones or a business like restaurants (Mary Bites or Mr. Biggs), as the owner of the company or business, is my duty to know the cost of the items and amount that will be produced out of the items been bought. The items that is used in baking or manufacturing the goods is called ingredient .Now after knowing the amount, you make your calculations of items cost price and amount produced, there you will know your cost and selling price of baked or manufactured products.

FORMULARS

- ITEMS = I   2. EACH = E

- CAPITAL = C   4. NUMBER = NO

- AMOUNT = AMT

- PACKET (CARTONS,BARREL & CHASET) = PACK

- TRANSPORTATION = T.P

Examples1: COMPANY: I owned a company that produces phones, and the ingredient of producing the phones are; Panel, battery, buttons, screen, camera and casing, these are the ingredient that makes up the phone. Am not manufacturing those component rather I bought them and produce my phone, let's say am manufacturing those component too, but there are basic ingredients that I'll put together to form those Component.

So, since I'll buy the component to produce my phones or the items to produce the component, I must know the cost of each item. Examples; panel pack =$30, battery pack =$40, screen pack =$10, camera's pack =$20, button pack = $20 and phone case pack =$40.

Now, my knowing the pack price alone, I will assume of knowing the cost price too, then I guess, my selling price too will be an assumption price, which means am band to fall in this my phones company because I'll be losing bits by bits till I completely loose out and my company collapses .So I must know how many are in each items pack to make my company successful and also grow in my business. So let's say Panel 10 pieces, battery 10 pieces, buttons 10 pieces, screen 10 pieces, camera 10 pieces and phone case 10 pieces, now that I now know the number of each items pack, I will make my calculation to know the cost price of each phone and know how to place my selling price.

ITEMS & PACKS I.C

ITEMS	PACKS I.C
PANEL	$30
BATTERY	$40
SCREEN	$10
CAMERA	$20
BUTTON	$20
PHONE CASE	$40

NUMBERS OF ITEMS CAPITAL (I.C)

NAMES OF ITEMS	NO OF E.I	AMT OF PACK I.C	CALCULATIONS	EACH I.C
PANEL	10	$30	$30 ÷ 10= $3	$3
BATTERY	10	$40	$40 ÷ 10= $4	$4

SCREEN	10	$10	$10 ÷ 10= $1	$1
CAMERA	10	$20	$20 ÷ 10= $2	$2
BUTTON	10	$20	$20 ÷ 10= $2	$2
PHONE CASE	10	$40	$40 ÷ 10= $4	$4

Now, I will make a division of T.P EXPENSES ÷ NO OF PRODUCED ITEM, to know the cost price addition to your expenses. And my total amount of expenditures is $4, why I produced 4 phones. There I can now know how to place my selling price, so that I will not be beaten by other companies or business, and my goods won't stay too long in my warehouse .so here I go with our calculations;

T.P EXPENSES ÷ PRODUCED ITEMS

T.P EXPENSES $4 ÷ 4 PHONES

(SO THEREFORE). $4 ÷ 4 =$1

$ 3 + $4 + $1 + $2 + $2 + $4=$16

$16 + $1 =$17.

Cost price =$17

The cost of each phone produced is $17.

So we now know the cost of each phone, we can now place our selling price that will make customers to be coming.

CHAPTER 3

Examples2: IMPORT & EXPORT: I owned a business (IMPORT & EXPORT) and am importing goods from other country to other country, and they are; Biscuit, Sugar, Milk, Milo and indomie, and I bought goods of $20 and my container just arrived. And when I opened it what I got was; Biscuit =10 cartons, Sugar =5 packets, Milk =20 cartons, Milo =5 cartons and Indomie =10 cartons. Now my calculations won't be in E.I.C (each items capital) but is in packs, cartons and in barrels(measurement) because I don't manufacture or produce ,but deals on packs, cartons and in barrel(measurement) ,as buyer and seller.

ITEMS & NUMBER OF E.I

ITEMS	NUBERS OF E.I
BUSCUIT	10
SUGAR	5
MILK	20
MILO	5
INDOMIE	10

NUMBERS OF PACKS I.C

NAME OF ITEMS	NUMBER OF E.I	CALCULATIONS	AMT OF E I.C
BUSCUIT	10	$20 \div 10 = \$2$	$2
SUGAR	5	$20 \div 5 = \$4$	$4
MILK	20	$20 \div \$20 = \$1$	$1
MILO	5	$20 \div 5 = \$4$	$4
INDOMIE	10	$20 \div 10 = \$2$	$2

Now, I will make a division of T.P EXPENSES ÷ NO OF PRODUCED ITEM, to know the cost price addition to my expenses. And my total amount of expenditures is $6; NUMBER OF PACK ITEMS is 5. There I can now know how to place my selling price. So here I go with our calculations;

T.P EXPENSES ÷ PRODUCED ITEMS

T.P EXPENSES $6 ÷ 5 ITEMS

(SO THEREFORE). $6 ÷ 5 = $1.12

AMT OF E.I.C + T.P EXPENSES

NAME OF ITEMS	CALCULATIONS OF AMT OF E.I.C +T.P EXPENSES	TOTAL AMT OF E I.C
BUSCUIT	$2 + $1.12 =$3.12	$3.12
SUGAR	$4 + $1.12 =$5.12	$5.12
MILK	$1 + $1.12 = $2.12	$2.12
MILO	$4 ÷ $1.12 =$5.12	$5.12
INDOMI E	$1 ÷ $1.12 =$2.12	$2.12

CHAPTER 4

Examples3: BAKING: I owned a restaurant business (Mary Bit's or Mr. Biggs) and I produce foods like soup & Garry, Rice and pepper soup, fried indomie, fried rice and chicken, pizza, cakes etc., for people to buy and eat. And am not manufacturing any of this ingredient (component) to make up my food for people to buy and eat, rather I bought them to use and prepare my food. Now I will use one of these items to calculate my business calculation.

So, since I'll buy my ingredient (component) to prepare my food, so I must know the cost of each item. Examples; PREPARATION OF CAKE, the ingredient of preparing a cake is;

Flour, sugar, nut milk, baking powder etc., and I bought 1 cup of flour = $5, 2 cups sugar = $8, nut milk = $2, baking powder = $3.

And after using my ingredient to bake my cake I come up with 3 cakes. The question there is, how do I know each cost price of cake

ITEMS & PACKS I.C

ITEMS	PACKS I.C
FLOUR	$5
SUGAR	$8
NUT MILK	$2
BAKING POWDER	$3

NUMBERS OF ITEMS CAPITAL (I.C)

NAMES OF ITEMS	NO OF E.I	AMT OF PACK I.C	CALCULATIONS	EACH I.C
FLOUR	1	$5	-----	$5
SUGAR	2	$8	$8 ÷ 2= $4	$4
NUT MILK	1	$2	-----	$2
BAKING POWDER	1	$3	------	$3

Now, I will make a division of T.P EXPENSES ÷ NO OF PRODUCED ITEMS, to know the cost price addition to my expenses. And my total amount of expenditures is $6, why I produced 3 cakes. There I can now know how to place my selling price .so I can now do my calculations;

T.P EXPENSES ÷ PRODUCED ITEMS

T.P EXPENSES $6 ÷ 3 CAKES

(SO THEREFORE). $6 ÷ 3 =$2

$5 + $4 + $2 + $3 =$14

$14 + $2 =$16.

Cost price =$16

The cost of each cake that I produced is $16.

So I now know the cost of each cake, I can now place my selling price that will make customers to be coming.

CHAPTER 5

Examples4: TRADES NATIONAL/LOCAL: I owned a business (TRADING) and am supplying goods and services to people around me and within the country. And they are; Biscuit, Sugar, Milk, Milo and indomie, and I bought goods of $20 and my container just arrived. And when I opened it, what I got was; Biscuit =10 cartons, Sugar =5 packets, Milk =20cartons, Milo =5 cartons and Indomie =10 cartons. Now my calculations won't be in E.I.C (each items capital) but is in packs, cartons and in barrels(measurement) because I don't manufacture or produce ,but deals on packs, cartons and in barrel(measurement) ,as buyer and seller.

ITEMS & NUMBER OF E.I

ITEMS	NUBER OF E.I
BUSCUIT	10
SUGAR	5
MILK	20
MILO	5
INDOMIE	10

NUMBERS OF PACK I.C

NAME OF ITEMS	NUMBER OF E.I	CALCULATIONS	AMT OF E I.C
BUSCUIT	10	$20 ÷ 10=$2	$2
SUGAR	5	$20 ÷ 5=$4	$4
MILK	20	20 ÷ $20 = $1	$1
MILO	5	$20 ÷ 5=$4	$4
INDOMIE	10	$20 ÷ 10=$2	$2

Now, I will make a division of T.P EXPENSES ÷ NO OF PRODUCED ITEMS, to know the cost price addition to my expenses. And my total amount of expenditures is $6; NUMBER OF PACK ITEMS is 5. There I can now know how to place my selling price .So here we go with our calculations;

T.P EXPENSES ÷ PRODUCED ITEMS

T.P EXPENSES $6 ÷ 5 ITEMS

(SO THEREFORE). $6 ÷ 5 =$1.12

AMT OF E.I.C + T.P EXPENCES

NAME OF ITEMS	CALCULATIONS OF AMT OF E.I.C +T.P EXPENSES	TOTAL AMT OF E I.C
BUSCUIT	$2 + $1.12 =$3.12	$3.12
SUGAR	$4 + $1.12 =$5.12	$5.12
MILK	$1 + $1.12 = $2.12	$2.12
MILO	$4 ÷ $1.12 =$4.12	$5.12
INDOMIE	$2÷ $1.12 =$2.12	$3.12

Since I now know the cost of each carton, and I want to know how many pieces are in each carton and there cost price, so I'll do my calculations to know the number and there cost price. And when I opened it, this is what I got; 10 pieces of Biscuit from 1 carton, 5 pieces of Sugar from 1 packet, 20 sachets of Milk from 1 carton, 5 sachets of Milo from 1 carton and 10 pieces of Indomie from 1 carton. Now my calculations must be in E.I.C (each items capital) because there lays my gain, and I deals on packs, cartons and in bottles (measurement) because I don't manufacture or produce, but I buy from wholesalers and importers.

ITEMS & NUMBER OF E.I

ITEMS	NUBER OF E.I
BUSCUIT	10
SUGAR	5
MILK	20
MILO	5
INDOMIE	10

NUMBERS OF ITEMS CAPITAL (I.C)

NAMES OF ITEMS	NO OF E.I	AMT OF PACK I.C	CALCULATIONS	EACH I.C
BISCUIT	10	$2	10 ÷ $2 = $5	$5
SUGAR	5	$4	5 ÷ $4= $1.25	$1.25
MILK	20	$1	20 ÷ $1 = $20	$20
MILO	5	$4	5 ÷ $4 =$1.25	$1.25
INDOMIE	10	$2	10 ÷ $2 = $5	$5

CHAPTER 6

MARKETING PRICE

MARKETING PRICE: These are the price made in our businesses and companies to market our products or goods. When talking about market price, we have two types of market price they are; cost price and selling price.

COST PRICE: these are total amount of fixed price used to buy your products or amount used to buy the ingredients or items used to produce a product.

SELLING PRICE: These are total amount fixed to market a product or goods, or any products produce in a business or company considering the cost price and gain.

EXAMPLE

COST PRICE	SELLING PRICE	
$50	PROFIT $30	SELLING PRICE
$20	$20 + $30 =$50	$50

So our selling price of each of the phone is $50.in this way you won't find it difficult to know you gain in your business or company.

CHAPTER 7

WORK SCHEDULE

WORK SCHEDULE: This is how to put in place or to regulate working hours, where to and how to work in a company or business (starting hours, closing hours, breaks time etc.) it is very very important to schedule your company or business because it will make you to know how many numbers of person needed for that area or numbers of worker needed to employ. Example, some company or business owner use one security man for day and night, is wrong because you're putting your worker and you yourself as the owner at risk, as well as the entire company or business in dangers, you know why? Because even health states that, is not good to over work the brain or the body, when someone over work the brain or the body he or she begins to misbehave. The moment you over work yourself it must have an effect, this effect in the aspect of business or company, crippled company or business, this things are the things that fall some company or business today. People usually say that over work make more gain, yes is true but not over labor someone but over work. Because if you over labor someone at the end of the day you will get yourself to be blame, because a little mistake will cripple that many years of over work. So if you want to over work in your company or business, you need to schedule your work according to the over work. Haven't you seen or experience, something you usually do every day, because you over work yourself you misbehave why doing it and you called it stress. Let's assume that is contracts, don't you think you have lost the contracts or crippled your company or business by signing in to wrong contract. Come to think of it, why do business or company owners take a day off or a week off whenever they are over worked even when there's contract to sign, rather they take it home for them to study or go through it. Telling the company to give them time to go through it.

MANAGER: Applicable to your manager to avoid misbehaviors in your company or business which can cause damage to your company or business someday.

WORKER: In the case of worker, the moment a worker over work his or herself in a company or business, you see that worker begin to misbehave in the aspect of manufacturing, baking, producing etc. and the items, goods or products loses it qualities or values because of short cut (to finish quick because of stress), in that act, the business or company collapse or cripple by losing their customers to other companies or business.

CHAPTER 8

SPLITION

SPLITION: This is the process or the way by which a company or business regulate his or her gain or profit to be used .They are; capital, maintainers, savings and usage. It is very necessary to split you gain because it will help a lot in your business or company to grow and stand firm in business or company crisis(high cost price, settlement of business customs, maintainers, transportations etc.) .

In a business or company we don't pray for anything to happen but paraphrase it happens how you tackle it, but with the help of splition you can tackle it, as well you will know how much you can use to tackle that problem and it won't affect the company or business.

Now there must be an instruction that the business or company owner must have for him or herself first, secondly, you alone must have the splition book as the owner of the company or business, thirdly you must have 4 to 5 account of the business or company you are running.

You might be wondering what are you going to do with all those accounts, or wondering if you are a fraudster or a hacker? The answer is no, you are none of these, but a company or business owner who is protecting his or herself, and to make his or her business grow and stand firm in terms of business or company crises.

- Accounts 1; you must have a general account for your company or business which will be known to all your workers and will be used for transactions

- Account 2; you must have your own 3 separate account for the company or business you are running, that will not be known to your workers.

In the splition there must be a maximum amount and minimum amount, which will regulate your usage both in the company or business and you.

REGULATION: In every $100, capital should first be removed. Every $50, a percentage of [$5 for maintainers, $10 for saving, any amount left is for use].But if the capital of E.I.C (each items capital) is $ 40 and above, then the remaining should go for usage.

EXAMPLES 1: I have 10 pieces of goods (panel =2, battery =2, screen =2, camera =2 and button =2), E.I.C = $20, E.S (each selling price) = $50. 27/ 5 / 20203 I sold 6 pieces of items.

SOLD ITEMS

ITEMS	AMOUNT
PANEL	$100
BATTERY	$50
SCREEN	$50
CAMERA	$50

BUTTON	$50

FROM SOLD ITEMS TO SPLITION

ITEMS	CAPITAL	MAINTAINERS	SAVINGS	USAGE
PANEL	$40	$10	$20	$30
BATTERY	$20	$5	$10	$15
SCREEN	$20	$5	$10	$15
CAMERA	$20	$5	$10	$15
BUTTON	$20	$5	$10	$15
TOTAL	$120	$30	$60	$90

EXAMPLES 2: i have 10 pieces of goods (panel =2, battery =2, screen =2, camera =2 and button =2), E.I.C = (panel= $40, battery =$20, camera =$30, screen = $20, button = $20, E.S (each selling price) =

$50. 27/ 5 / 20203 I sold 6 pieces of items.

SOLD ITEMS

ITEMS	AMOUNT
PANEL	$50
BATTERY	$50
SCREEN	$50
CAMERA	$100
BUTTON	$50

FROM SOLD ITEMS TO SPLITION

ITEMS	CAPITAL	MAINTAINERS	SAVINGS	USAGE
PANEL	$40	$0	$0	$10
BATTERY	$20	$5	$10	$15

SCREEN	$20	$5	$10	$15
CAMERA	$60	$5	$10	$25
BUTTON	$20	$5	$10	$15
TOTAL	$160	$20	$40	$80

As I told you earlier with this you will overcome business or company crisis. There comes in the 3 account to play, each of this splition must have an account to run with to avoid mistakes, apart from the capital account which is the general account.

MAINTAINERS: When we are talking about maintainer we are not just talking about when generator got spoil or when instrument got spoil but we are also talking about anything that go against the company or business target or focus. Like high cost price, settlement of business customs, maintainers, transportations etc.

Maintainers should be fix on maximum and minimum rate, like maximum rate = $10m, minimum rate = $5m. Now anything above the maximum rate should be put in usage, then anything less than the minimum rate of the maintainers, the percentage should continue again.

SAVINGS: We all know what savings is, it's a life time gathering or life time investment in a particular business or company, so it won't have any maximum or minimum rate but continue it percentage savings.

USAGE: This is monthly usage or accidental serve as personal usage in a company. Now it has a big role to play in the company or business, that is why it percentage is the biggest of all, the big role it has to play; is worker's salary and personal salary. For example at the end of the month your monthly usage is $6m, then your workers salary should be paid in that money.

REMEMBER

THIS STRATEGIES WILL NOT OCCUR BY ITSELF UNTILL YOU TAKE OR MAKE A BOLD STEP.

"ACTION MAKES THE DIFFERENCE"

PLEASE NOTE:
DOWNLOAD THESE BOOKS THAT WORK TOGETHER WITH THIS BOOK
1*) WORK BOOK OF [THE HIDDEN SECRET OF SUCCESSFUL INTERNATIONAL BUSINESSES & COMPANIES]
2*) SPLITION WORK BOOK OF [THE HIDDEN SECRET OF SUCCESSFUL INTERNATIONAL BUSINESSES & COMPANIES]

ABOUT THE AUTHOR

Chris Thankgod

Chris Thankgod is a business mentor and developer that teaches and groom all kinds of businesses to the expected or required stage of the business owner

In this book Chris Thankgod teaches business owners to know the strategies of making 100 – 500 Trillion, Billions, Millions and Thousands in your currency and as well in Dollar's in a day. Chris Thankgod teach you how to embark on a business you don't know with the little ideas you have and how to run your business without being cheated and your goods not to stay too long in a ware-house or store.